HOW MANY EDENS

Conjures a garden where no garden is
-Donald Justice from "Southern Gothic"

Janice Silverman Rebibo

How Many
Edens

Coolidge Corner Publishing

In memory of Lewie, my first Adam.

Acknowledgments:

Author photo by Liz Linder Photograpy.

Special thanks to the editors of *Soul-Lit* and *Muddy River Poetry Review*
for online periodical publication of a number of my recent poems and to
Joel Moskowitz, Linda Goldberg, Zvi Sesling, Deborah Leipziger and
Amos Levitan for reading these *Eden* poems along with me as they came
into being.

This book's opening poems, *Longing and Loathing* and *How Many Edens
Have I Known*, were written and shared at the *2013 Soul-Lit Spiritual Poetry
Retreat*, held at the Providence Zen Center in Cumberland, RI. They were
first published in the Fall 2013 issue of *Soul-Lit*

Coolidge Corner Publishing

info@coolidgecornerpublishing.com

How Many Edens

Poems

LONGING AND LOATHING

We were in my Garden of Eden
When he said the sweetest thing
Naked on my dayglo white
King-sized bed
At the edge of my tiny meadow
Where the grass had gone all to seed
In the shade of the knowledge trees.
Biblically dappled sunlight
Graced his loins, I mean,
Made his skin look awfully
Good
to me.
"This is not new," is what he said,
"and I don't think you should be
Zen about anything."

HOW MANY EDENS HAVE I KNOWN

How many Edens have I known
Walking up the stony path
Rejuvenated by a memory
Of dust and potato peels
Our pond is bluer than the sky

SEMI-FORMAL IN THE GROVE

Semi-formal in the grove,
they spoke in strong verbs
and melodious parts of speech.
Depending on the day,
she was his rib,
he had her back
to back to back.
Simplistically, they took
their shape from oak leaves,
their favorite flavor was tomato –
that amorous, bulbous fruit,
there were no surprises even then.

HEMINGWAY WROTE 800 PAGES

Hemingway wrote 800 pages on the Garden of Eden.
Disney, like Collodi, used a conman fox instead
of a serpent. His antagonist, this Foulfellow, sold
Pinocchio to God, the impresario Stromboli – a
puppeteer named after a pastry named after a volcano.
Who was Eve's God in Eden on her author's carpet?
Editor and author. Persian carpet on his study floor.

A GARDEN OF HERBACEOUS PLANTS

Paradise Is Just Where You Are Right Now
-Dieter Kienast (after Laurie Anderson)

An ideogram for Paradise
is a field of
broken pots.
At the end of days
when all the shards
rise up and recombine, divine
remediation by means of
landfill and
lightfill
will bear witness to our cityscapes.
She will spy him once again
silhouetted against a wall of glass.
A garden is just where we are
right now. Spin around. The continual
juxtaposition of town and country stirs up
this torpid pool. This is no sterile photo
of a conceptual landscape. The chair
is empty because he stood up
to take her in his arms.

HOMONYM

The Garden of Eden
is an inspirational story
like an Australian movie
about an Olympic hopeful
swimmer who chooses
Harvard instead, a homonym
or, if you prefer, like
a novel that ends with
the couple driving off
together in a taxi
but submerged in what is.

GRAFFITI ON THE GARDEN WALL

THERE IS ONLY ONE ADAM
           or at least one at a time
                   most of the time

ETERNAL TRIANGLE

Though
it took Him
what seemed like
forever to make His
first move, once He did
no main-man Adam ever stood
a chance up against His handful of
lustrous fruit from His fabled kumquat
tree and one of His powerful, upright hugs.
Whenever He'd phone she'd drop everything and run.

GOING OUT FROM THE PRESENCE

Feet-high steeplebush-spikes and loosestrife
magenta along the river after he lectured
tripping the light fantastic across the stage
explicating Lensky's small poem about a lost
home, its few words projected on a cinematic
screen. Violet swamp verbena. Creeping purple
morning glory vines and profuse magenta-pink
and lavender rhododendra in the rain. Then
to her New England lake where he pronounced
gently that he was "at the end of the turn," and
gestured toward the path that curved around the
bend of her local puddle in the haze. "Remember
this moment," although he'd go forth and live
and write among the thorns and thistles for another
forty years as they say.

ONE OF OUR HOLY CITIES

The bus door opened
at the first stop
at the entrance to the town
known for its hot springs.
I cannot describe
the color of his shirt
the color of a dream
the sixtieth portion of prophecy.

ALL THE ILLS OF THE EARTH

"Almost all the ills of the earth remain in the title. Beyond, without, on the other side of the garden wall!" he railed.
"This allows us to concentrate on what is within, what is immanent, the local events," she countered.
"Like pie tasting," he smirked.
"And the insufferable three-legged races that run regularly within these confines," rolling her eyes.
"Darling, it is not all sweetness," he winked.
"Yes, let's cast off that male assumption. It is a psychosocial ecosystem like any other," she sighed.

WHY THE MAN WAS DRIVEN OUT

1.
He was having sex
with that snake
in the shower.
And let us set
the record straight –
the serpent in this
version is a she.
The woman we call
Eve was asleep
in the next room.
The shower stall in
question was free-
standing. Eve
heard it lurch
and her eyes
were opened.

2.
He barely motioned
with his hand apologetically,
signaling "This is it," to her
from his easy chair
across the room
with his intimate,
quizzical eyes.
Mortality was not so much
a question of performance
as of function. Of being
bone tired.

3.
The next to the last time the
Woman saw one of her earlier
Adams, she was driving
in reverse – backing away
from him at breakneck speed,
backing out of his overlong,
unpaved driveway.
She drove herself
out of that garden estate
while a purportedly
more authentic Eve
beheld the scene
from their floral threshold.
As she flew, the reversing
Woman twisted her head
once to look through
her front windshield
back at the Man. She
did not turn to stone
or become a pillar of salt
from the glimpse she caught
of His brimstone and fire
raining down on her secret desire.
The next time she saw Adam,
he had a blanket on his knees.

YOUR NEXT EDEN

To the extent that every one of us is damaged en route
between then and now, we are called upon to rebuild
the illusion of a paradise each time we fall – as if

the circle of our lives inscribes a square – to deck those
four walls again with the identical garlands of irrelevant
sonnets and roses that are never really there – to conjure,

using any means we can, a sacred space for a mythical
woman and man. The greater the extent of the damage
sustained in the journey from conception to here and now,
the more perfect will be your Eden until the next time

you fall. A fall is a slip, not a sin. To the extent that
time and strength permit, you'll most likely rise up
and sing again, circumscribing your next Eden with
ring upon ring upon ring of roses.

Author's Notes

How Many Edens grew from seeds planted by Professor and
Chaplain Wayne-Daniel Berard in his sessions at the Summer 2013
Soul-Lit Poetry Retreat held at the Providence Zen Center. A brief text-
study of passages from Genesis along with his past life regression
visualization "conjured a garden" for me. In this poem cycle, you will
find a few allusions, direct and less so, to biblical and rabbinic sources,
Most are well-known. Perhaps less familiar are the phrases "thorns and
thistles", in *Going Out from the Presence* on p.10, taken from Genesis
3:18 and, in *One of Our Holy Cities* on p.11, "...a dream / the sixtieth
portion of prophecy," from the Talmud (*Berachot* 57b). *Longing and
Loathing,* the title of the first poem, is an allusion to Soren Kierkegaard's
Fear and Trembling, based on the *Akeda* (Genesis 22:1-22:19).

Dieter Kienast (1945-1998) was a Swiss landscape architect –
inspiring, quirky and ecologically savvy. The motto for my poem
A Garden of Herbaceous Plants – "Paradise Is Just Where You Are Right
Now" – appears in enormous letters on a wall curving through a sketch I
saw of Kienast's design for the Moabiter Werder Park in Berlin. I later
discovered that Keinast's words were a garden artist's sly response to
"Paradise is exactly like where you are right now only much much better,"
a key line from American performance artist Laurie Anderson's 1986 UK
hit song, *Language Is a Virus.* My thanks to Amos Levitan for countering
with a saying by Hasidic Master Rabbi Nachman of Bratslev (sometimes
attributed to another). It is based on the passage from the story of the
Burning Bush in Exodus (3:5), echoed in Joshua (5:15), dealing with
revelation and even miracles: "...the place where you are standing is
holy ground." המקום אשר אתה עומד עליו אדמת קודש הוא Loosely, the
Hasidic saying suggests that the ground may be sanctified anywhere you
are and that wherever you find yourself right now is the place you were
meant to deal with. In the same poem, "stirs up this torpid pool" alludes to
30-year-old T. S. Eliot's comment about Boston in his letter to Isabella
Stuart Gardner, 7 November 1918.

The last line of *Your Next Eden* was inspired by the last line of
Southern Gothic by Donald Justice, from which the motto of this book is
taken.

Janice Silverman Rebibo is the author of five previous books of poetry and a volume of translations to English of the selected work of beloved Israeli poet Natan Yonatan, *Within the Song to Live*. *My Beautiful Ballooning Heart*, her collected English poetry, was released by Coolidge Corner Publishing in July 2013.

Rebibo's poems have been described as "fresh and compelling", having "an intriguing sense of humor", and showing "just how globally oriented the world has become". Her poem, "My Beautiful Ballooning Heart", was nominated by *Muddy River Poetry Review* for a 2012 Pushcart Prize.

A Massachusetts native and native English speaker, Rebibo received a President of Israel award and others for *Zara Betzion* [a stranger-woman in Zion], *Poems 1984-2006*, her collected Hebrew poetry. Israeli critics called her work "a bold blend of two imposing literary traditions" and "a strategic breakthrough that added something new to the war of independence of Israel's consciousness."

For more details, please visit www.janicerebibo.com.

www.ingramcontent.com/pod-product-compliance
Lightning Source LLC
Chambersburg PA
CBHW060550030426
42337CB00021B/4519